Index

NOTE : Index will help to find what you're looking for easily . but in order to make it super easy and fun for you, we have organized the themes as follows : each theme has 5 pages without counting the blank ones. the first 3 pages are for photos, the Fourth page is for quotes and the Fifth one is for affirmations and power words.

What is a Vision Board ?

A vision board is a tool used to help clarify, concentrate and maintain focus on what truly matters to you. Literally, a vision board is any sort of board on which you display images that represent whatever you want to be, do or have in your life.

Do vision boards really work ?

The visual stimulation experienced as a result of looking at your board on a daily basis will strengthen your emotional connection to achieving your goals and as a result, start showing you how you will come to accomplish your grandest desires. A picture truly is worth a thousand words.

Vision Boards and the Law of Attraction

A vision board is a powerful way to engage the subconscious mind and Law of Attraction to make your goals and desires attainable. by creating a vision board, you're telling your subconscious mind what you want to focus on.

Law of Attraction experts call it the act of Visualization .

Visualization is one of the most powerful techniques you can apply into your life to manifest your desires and reach your goals.

How to Create A Vision Board That Actually Works

STEP 1: HAVE CLARITY

Before even starting your board, it's crucial to first set intentions and develop clarity about what kind of life you're really looking for. Here are some questions to help get you started:

- ❯ When I am living my ideal life, I want to feel...
- ❯ I want to learn more of...
- ❯ A day in my life looks like...
- ❯ My definition of success is...
- ❯ I feel like myself when...

Really spend some time and jot down your answers with as much detail as possible. The more specific you are about what kind of life you really want, the easier it will be for you to set goals and take actions to achieve them.

STEP 2: CREATE A VISION BOARD

Key elements for creating a powerful vision board:

Visuals: Images, pictures, symbols that align with your goals and the vision of you in your ideal state of Being.

Power Words: These might change over time, but they carry with them the true meaning about who you are at the core. They might be your values or words that inspire you. Example: Health, Love, Happiness, Community, Adventure

Quotes: Your favorite quotes or sayings that inspire you to be the best and most energized you..

Affirmations: A statement that is framed as already being true about you, regardless of your present circumstances. For example "I am worthy of my dreams". "I am vibrantly healthy and thriving inside my beautiful body."

To begin, find pictures that symbolize the experiences, things, and feelings you want to attract into your life. Begin cutting them out. Organize your words and images neatly on a board that is big enough to fit your needs, 3 feet by 2 feet is pretty standard.

Once your board is complete put it in a place that you can easily view it in the morning upon awakening and at night before you fall asleep. If you built a vision board for your business then consider placing it in your office where you can look at it throughout the day and use it as a source of inspiration to keep you going.

Tools and Supplies for Creating a Vision Board

> Scissors and Glue Stick
> List of your goals
> Pictures, Quotes..... that inspire you
> A Board: Your vision board can be built on a piece of cardboard, corkboard or vintage wood.

Like all new things in life, the most challenging part of creating your vision board is simply starting. **Take your first step right after reading this .**

STEP 3: LOOK AT YOUR BOARD DAILY

After clearly defining your goals and creating a vision board to support them, we suggest you implement a daily routine for reviewing your goals and visualizing what life is like having already attained your grandest desires.

This simple exercise helps to program your subconscious mind to continue working on your goals even when you are at rest or working on other activities and it only takes 10 minutes.

➤ Sit calmly in front of your vision board for 2-3 minutes. Let your board inspire you.

➤ Close your eyes for 2-3 minutes and visualize yourself living the life you have always imagined or achieved the goals you wish to aim for in the months to come. Paint pictures in your mind.

➤ Read your goals out loud to yourself.

➤ Write down 2-3 things you are grateful for you in your life that already support your vision. These could be as simple as breathing or the time you took to invest in this visualization exercise.

Let your light Shine

TAKE CARE OF YOURSELF

Prevent Care Love

YOU got This

live laugh love

Rise and Shine

I treat myself with compassion.

**I AM
LIGHTENING
MY LOAD.**

`I CHERISH THE TIME`
`I TAKE TO REFILL.`

I believe in who I am.

BEAUTY

SELF
CARE

RELAX

POSITIVE
VIBES

18

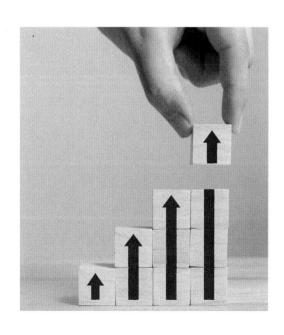

There is only one way to avoid criticism: Do nothing, say nothing, and be nothing.

Right this moment
I am attracting the
perfect career into
my life

MY CAREER
HAPPINESS
IS MY
CHOICE.

RIGHT NOW, THE JOB
I AM LOOKING FOR IS
LOOKING FOR ME!

Career

believe →

Grateful

dream →

hope

GOOD BOOKS
&
GOOD COMPANY

Money is like muck—not good unless it be spread

" If you would be wealthy, think of saving as well as getting. "

" Time is more valuable than money. You can get more money, but you cannot get more time. "

DREAM BIG, WORK HARD, MAKE IT happen.

I CAN I WILL

I use money to better my life and the lives of others.

I AM WORTHY OF MAKING MORE MONEY.

I CONSTANTLY ATTRACT OPPORTUNITIES THAT CREATE MORE MONEY.

Money

WEALTH

RICH

Time

CASH

35

Will you be mine?
YOU MAKE
ME HAPPY

I need You like a heart needs a beat

It's always better when we're together.

" EVERY TIME I SEE YOU, I FALL IN LOVE ALL OVER AGAIN. "

My night has become a sunny dawn because of you.

I am grateful for the love in my life.

I LOVE WHO I AM, AND SO DOES MY PARTNER.

I AM WORTHY OF A HEALTHY, LOVING RELATIONSHIP.

LOVE

Real Love

ROMANTIC

HIM

ATTRACTION

48

" A room without books is like a body without a soul "

" He who asks is a fool for five minutes, but he who does not ask remains a fool forever "

" People learn more on their own rather than being force fed "

" They know enough who know how to learn "

" Learning is a treasure that will follow its owner everywhere "

I easily remember everything that I read.

MY MIND IS EXPANDING EACH DAY.

MY BRAIN CAN EASILY CONTAIN
A LOT OF INFORMATION.

Education

Educated

Discovering

Devised

"Spiritual progress is like a detoxification"

The spiritual life does not remove us from the world but leads us deeper into it

"Be guided by spirit and not driven by ego."

Your sacred space is where you can find yourself over and over again.

Take care of your inner, spiritual beauty. That will reflect in your face

Today I am centered in my heart, and closer to Spirit.

SPIRIT IS ALWAYS WITH ME, GUIDING ME.

I RESPECTFULLY ASK FOR DIVINE GUIDANCE IN ALL AREAS OF MY LIFE.

Spirituality

Correction

Truth

Prayer

Profound

Peace

Faith

Family is not an important thing. It's everythin

No matter what happens, a family will always have your back.

Once a mother, always a mother.

A family is the purest form of love and acceptance.

Your family will always hold your heart.

We build each other up, not tear each other down

OUR FAMILY IS BLESSED AND HIGHLY FAVORED

WE ARE WHOLE, HEALTHY, AND WALKING IN THE FULLNESS OF OUR PURPOSES

Family

Adoring

affectionate

Cohesive

Warm

76

"Let food be thy medicine and medicine be thy food"

"An apple a day keeps the docter away"

Every negative belief weakens the partnership between mind and body.

It is health that is the real wealth, and not pieces of gold and silver.

I have all the energy I need to accomplish my goals.

I APPRECIATE AND LOVE MY BODY

MY SLEEP IS RELAXED AND REFRESHING.

I choose to be at a healthy weight

Health

Nutrition

WORKOUT

ENERGY

88

90

"I haven't been everywhere, but it's on my LIST"

"You don't have to be rich to travel well"

Oh the places you'll go.

{ Investment in travel is an investment in yourself }

Travel far enough, you meet yourself

I am deeply fortunate
to be in the position to
travel.

TRAVEL MAKES
ME AN
OPTIMIST.

TRAVEL CULTIVATES
CHEER IN ME EVERY DAY.

I am the architect of
my travel fortune.

Journey

Arrive

Travel

Discover

GO

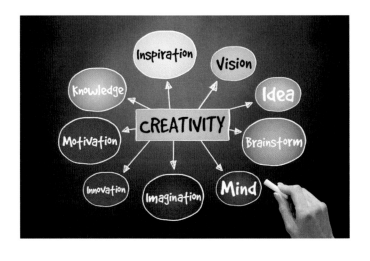

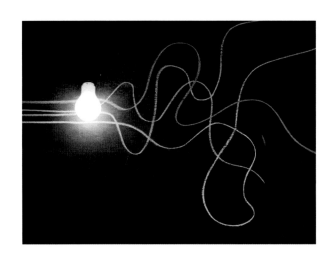

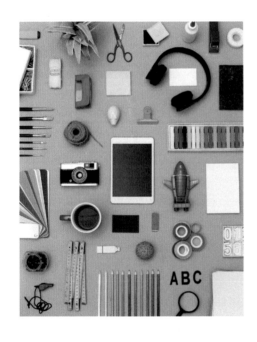

Creativity is intelligence having fun

The creative adult is the child who survived

"Create with the heart; build with the mind"

"Have no fear of perfection, you'll never reach it"

I always develop new ways to do things.

MY IDEAS ARE INNOVATIVE AND USEFUL.

NEW ORIGINAL IDEAS COME TO ME FREELY AND EASILY.

I increase my ingenuity in everything I do.

Creativity

Imagination

Create

originality

IDEA

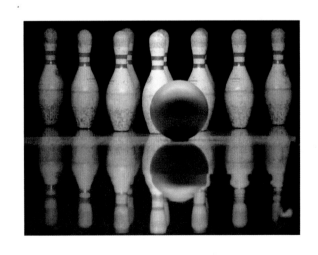

Make a commitment to having fun. See your best friends and make time for your hobbies and passions.

Sometimes you don't need to work or even to learn. you just need to have fun

"Some Days Are Simply Made For Playing."

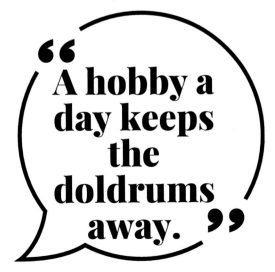

" A hobby a day keeps the doldrums away. "

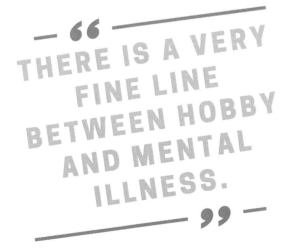

— " —
THERE IS A VERY FINE LINE BETWEEN HOBBY AND MENTAL ILLNESS.
— " —

I give myself
permession to
have fun

I LEARN
NEW SKILLS
EASILY

I control how I spend my time.

fun

HOBBY

leisure

Pleasure

Pastime

Recreation

Passion

How was your experience with our book ?

We would be very grateful
if you could leave us a review!